Strategy Games

A collection of 50 games & puzzles to stimulate mathematical thinking

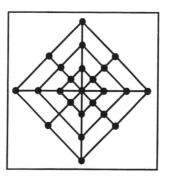

*If puzzles are posed
and children are curious,
then ...
possibilities can be explored ...
problems defined ...
patterns sought ...
perseverance developed ...
progress shared ...
pathways recorded ...
pleasure found ...
and playing becomes learning!*

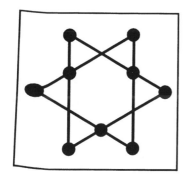

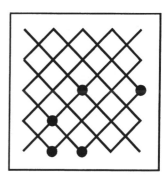

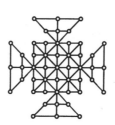

Reg Sheppard   John Wilkinson

Tarquin Group
www.tarquingroup.com

Introduction

Because they lend themselves to investigations at varying levels, many of the games and puzzles included in this collection are suitable for use with children of quite a wide range of ability and knowledge. Thoughtful use of games like these can broaden and enrich a child's mathematical experience, while providing opportunities for co-operative problem solving and for original thinking. We also hope that they will be enjoyed!

The games and puzzles in this collection require children to look for patterns and relationships while encouraging the development of ideas about number, space, tessellations, shapes, boundaries and networks. Players are encouraged to communicate their findings and to express them precisely in symbols.

We have included versions of many traditional games from around the world, together with a number specially devised with our purposes in mind. *Point Four* and *Interrupt*, which have their origins in traditional Japanese games, are played on the coordinate plane and should help children to become more confident about graphical work. The patterns of *Achi* and its related games or *The Circles of Hanoi* offer opportunities to identify and compare mathematical structures. Exploration of *Star Track* and *Pentagram* should help to develop understanding of infinite number systems as well as providing an approach to the notion of the inverse. In solving *Frogs*, children may realise the benefit of starting with a simpler situation and then applying the pattern discovered step by step to a more complex problem.

Some of the traditional games may be of particular interest during project work, in particular cross-curriculum and multi-cultural studies. There are games from Ancient Egypt, West Africa, the Viking lands, Spain, India, Japan, China, Tibet, Korea, Sri Lanka and New Zealand. In particular, *Wari,* a game which was played in Ancient Egypt, is still known in various versions throughout southern Africa and Asia. It is a good example of a game which requires counting and planning skills.

We think that too many packs of educational games rely on the use of dice as a game procedure. The emphasis in this collection is on the encouragement of thinking about strategies and the random factor introduced by dice is best avoided. These games need nothing extra for their playing except a few counters - and lively minds. Similarly, none of the games need much computation as we believe that there are already plenty of number games devised by teachers to meet the need for number bond practice.

There is no straightforward progression of difficulty throughout this collection. However, the games within each small group are presented in the order of increasing complexity. Any part of this book may be freely copied within the school purchasing it, but these copies may not be used for commercial purposes.

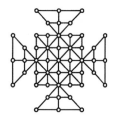

© 2002:   Reg Sheppard, John Wilkinson
© 1989:   First Edition

ISBN 9780906212707
Printed and Distributed in the USA by IPG:
www.ipgbook.com

Tarquin
Suite 74, 17 Holywell Hill
St Albans AL1 5JR UK
www.tarquingroup.com

Contents

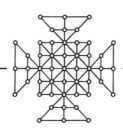

Suggestions, Strategies and Solutions

Children may be drawn into new challenges as a result of playing the games or tackling the puzzles. . .

'What are the winning strategies (or losing routes)?'
'Can the first (or second) player ensure a win?'
'How many steps are needed to solve this puzzle?'
'Why do you think that this problem has no solution?'
'Can you make a prediction about this game, and then test it?'
'Can you invent a simpler version of this game, in order to explore its structure?'
'Can you make a generalisation about this kind of game?'
'How did the breakthrough come?'
'Can you record the stages your thinking went through?'
'Can you find a better way to record the pattern of moves?'
'Can you invent an interesting new game, using what you have discovered?'

The Games

Number Bond Games

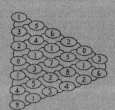

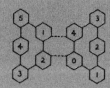

TARGET   **TOTAL**   **SUMMITS**

1

TARGET
This game is not self-correcting, and children might make unrecognised errors whilst playing – a rather common feature of number activities. However, players are encouraged to challenge any answers they believe to be wrong. An extra safeguard – and good practice anyway – is the requirement that children record each step, e.g. $3 + 1 = 4$ $4 + 5 = 9$ $9 + 1 = 10$ etc.

The rule 'No space may be used twice' may be adopted.

2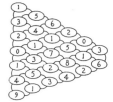

TOTAL
This time, 'looking ahead' is called for, as choices at each step are limited – and grow fewer as the game progresses. An electronic version of this game requires that a digit button on a calculator may only be chosen if it is adjacent to the previous one pressed. The 'zero' button is excluded.

3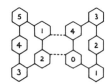

SUMMITS
This game provides fewer options still, but a greater opportunity to anticipate moves and thus to control the course of the game. Moves may be recorded.

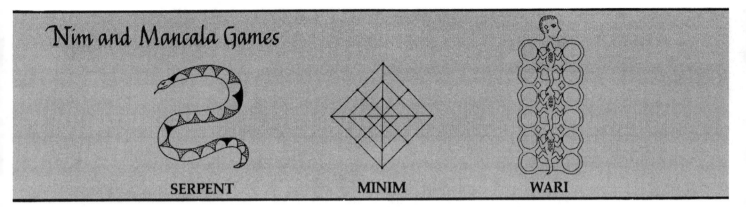

Nim and Mancala Games

SERPENT   **MINIM**   **WARI**

In the ancient game of Nim, two players would take turns to remove one or two counters from a pile, the last to play being the loser (or winner, if agreed beforehand).

With children, begin with a very simple game – just seven counters would be enough – in which they can begin to develop their ideas of strategies, and get some practice in rapid simple computation.

If four counters are left, the player who must take either one or two counters can be forced in his or her next turn to take the last one. Take the argument further: If there are seven counters at the start, note that whatever the first player takes, the second player can reduce the number remaining to four . . . It is now clear that the second player can always win this seven counter Nim. Using more counters, the children will be able to discover the key series . . . 13, 10, 7, 4, 1. If M = maximum counters taken in one turn, then the second player can ensure that M + 1 is taken each round. Only if the initial number is a multiple of M + 1, plus one counter extra, can second player be sure of a win – otherwise the first player can set up a win by a correct first move.

Another version of Nim permits the removal of any number of counters from any one pile, where several piles exist. A scheme based on binary arithmetic provides a way of ensuring a win. The 'safe' player checks that after his or her turn, there will be left an even number of any binary groups present in the piles. For instance, in the simple and traditional form beginning with piles of three, four and five counters, the analysis is as follows:

		Eights	Fours	Twos	Units
Number of counters in pile:	3			1	1
	4		1		
	5		1		1
		(Even)	(Even)	(Odd)	(Even)

There is only one set of two, so this must be removed to make the game 'safe'. Whatever the other player removes, the 'safe' player is always in a position to restore the balance of binary groups until the final few moves, when the tactic depends on whether the game is for a last player win or loss.

4

SERPENT
Explore the game using one counter, remembering that in this form of Nim the last to play, wins. How many spaces should a player try to leave available after his or her turn? Children may discover that the key series this time is 16, 12, 8, 4, 0. However, once several counters are in play, blocking moves become possible. . . and analysis much more difficult.

5

MINIM
Move from the linear game of Serpent to the two-dimensional array of Minim. This game is too complicated for complete analysis, and therefore continuous scoring is suggested so that there can be purposeful play even in the early stages. (One point gained per counter removed, but five points lost for taking the final one). 'Thinking back' from the final move should be encouraged.

Minim can also be played on a three-dimensional Noughts-and-Crosses board.

6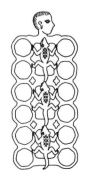

WARI
Wari also involves progressive removal of counters from a common set, but in this game (once played in Ancient Egypt and still very popular in Africa and Asia) the playing board is divided into two zones, one belonging to each player. There are many variants of Wari or Mancala; in each of them, a turn involves the sowing of counters round a board and the possibility of removing counters from the final cell reached. The game rules usually provide for counters to be taken from preceding cells too, but we offer here a simplified version.

In the modern race game of Backgammon (derived from the ancient Roman game of Tabula), each player has separate counters, and dice are used to limit the range of moves. Nevertheless, an affinity with Wari is apparent in such tactics as attacks on vulnerable pieces and the defensive grouping of home counters.

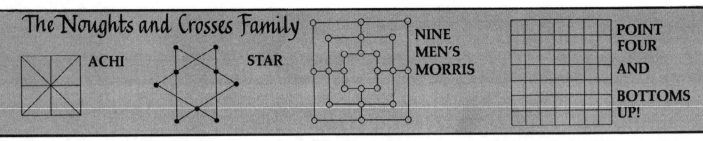
Mathematicians are interested in studying and classifying structures, and are intrigued when they find similar patterns in what had at first appeared to be quite different systems. Such parallel instances are said to show 'isomorphism'.

For the first eight moves, Achi is just like Noughts-and-Crosses; if the game of Achi is played with five counters each and no movement of counters once played, the similarity is complete.

7

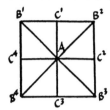

ACHI

How many alternative opening moves are there? How many second, third, fourth moves. . .? The first nine moves can each be followed by any of eight second moves, and so on. The total number of possible combinations of nine moves filling the board is 9! (factorial), i.e. 9 x 8 x 7 x 6 x 5 x 4 x 3 x 2 x 1. But does it make any real difference if the game begins at one corner rather than another? Children may discover that rotations or reflections reduce the number of distinct opening moves to just three (A, B and C in the diagram). How many lines does each of these moves affect? (Four, three and two respectively) So, which is the strongest opening play?

How many distinct combinations of two moves are there? They may find:

A B (any B)   A C (any C)   B A;   B B (adjacent);   B B (opposite);   B C (adjacent);   B C (distant)   C A; C B (adjacent);   C B (distant);   C C (adjacent);   C C (opposite) – making twelve combinations unless the sequence of moves is disregarded, in which case there are only eight distinct patterns.

Since Achi does not have a nine-move limit, a thoughtful player needs to anticipate possible moves beyond the ninth move, when counters are slid to new positions. Noughts-and-Crosses should always be a drawn game, but is this true of Achi? Incidentally, both games have eight winning lines, three playing points per line, and nine playing points in all (8, 3, 9).

8

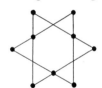

STAR

Now introduce Star. Is Star isomorphic with Achi? Why not? Star has six lines, three playing points per line, and nine playing points in all (6, 3, 9). How many lines does each point affect? Try to invent another game with a 6, 3, 9 pattern . . .

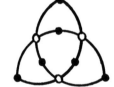

Here is ROTOR. A winning line of three must lie on a single arc, and the central point of a winning line must be a white dot. Each arc has five points; there are six winning lines, each using three playing points, and nine playing points in all . . .

Some other variations of the Noughts-and-Crosses family are:

FORCE

Reverse Noughts-and-Crosses; a player completing a line, loses.

DONKEY

A version of Force in which a player may play either colour counter (nought or cross) at each move. The object is to trap one's opponent into completing a line.

TICTACTOE

On the Achi or Twos Across board, players take turns to place their own three counters. Play then continues by sliding moves until a line of three is achieved, but the moves must be orthogonal (along a row or column, not diagonal).

To record moves in any of these games, children will need to devise a way to label the playing board.

9

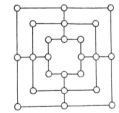

NINE MEN'S MORRIS

Nine Men's Morris was played 3500 years ago in Ancient Egypt, also in Troy, in Bronze Age Ireland . . . A game board was even found in the Gokstad ship in Norway (a.d. 900). This game has sixteen possible winning lines, each with three playing points, and twenty-four points in all. Which points are the most important? (Which points control movement from one circuit to another?) Children may observe that certain points on the network allow four directions of movement, whilst some of the others allow only two.

Twelve Men's Morris is played on a board where each set of three corner points is also linked by a diagonal line.

10

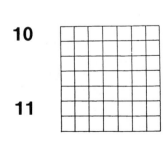

POINT FOUR

When played using a blackboard or overhead projector, this game is suitable for a class activity in which children dictate moves to a child acting as team marker. This offers practice in the co-ordinate system, using ordered pairs. The x axis reference (bottom line of numerals) is given first – Just as for map references, the 'Easting' precedes the 'Northing'.

11

BOTTOMS UP!

Is it advantageous to play first?

Are centrally placed counters more likely to figure in a winning line? If so, why is this? (A corner can only figure in three possible lines, whereas the central space might by used in any of

12

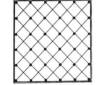

INTERRUPT

Make it clear that a continuous, but not necessarily straight, line is required from edge to edge in order to win. Corner points may be used for either winning line.

Which player has the advantage?

Which playing points are the most important? The tactics of this game may be explored first on smaller boards. The game becomes more interesting when some diagonal links are included; otherwise, drawn games soon become inevitable as players learn blocking tactics.

With too many diagonals on a tiny board, a simple first player win becomes obvious. On the larger board, blocking the more restricted parts of the opponent's route, without wasting any moves which do not contribute to one's own progress, is the way to proceed. Children should soon be able to discover how to take advantage of the alternative route that a diagonal branch offers.

13

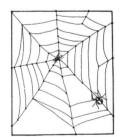

EXCHANGE KONO

Related as it is to the Victorian game of Halma, this game is a little more subtle than it at first appears – There are actually two interlacing networks, and each counter can move over only half of the playing points, like a Bishop in Chess.

14

A PARLOUR GAME

Which is the spider's best first move? Children may soon realise that the spider should patrol the perimeter of the web rather than chase across the web after the insect. Which is the most direct route to the window frame for the insect? Can it be caught?

15

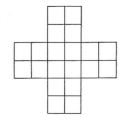

CATTLE DRIVE

This collection includes several ancient games, such as Fox & Geese, Kungser, and Cows & Leopards, in which contests are fought between two unequal or dissimilar forces. Cattle Drive is a simpler version in which children can explore the tactics for blocking moves.

16

FOX AND GEESE

Children studying a historical topic about the Vikings will enjoy playing in a Viking game tournament. Other traditional games can be used to add vitality to children's studies in the same kind of way.

The geese have the advantage, and can force a win without losing any pieces or even moving backward. Games can be tried with fewer geese, or even two foxes.

In this particular collection, Fox & Geese is the first to involve capture of opposing pieces by the 'jumping over' move.

Exploring Tessellations and Game Board Networks

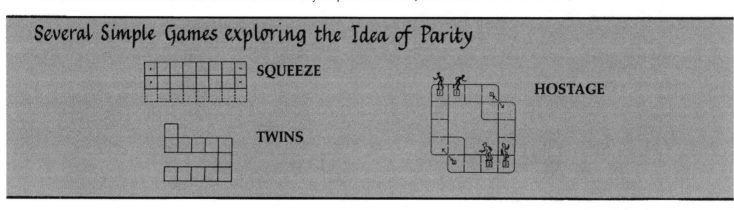

HEXA

CONTRAST

17

HEXA (and HEXNAKES)

After the introductory game, the rules may be extended to allow play on a space where two adjacent hexagons are already occupied. Now snakes and rings appear instead of mere pairs of occupied spaces. Children can try to discover the patterns which lead to minimum and maximum numbers of counters having been placed in a completed game using these rules.

HEXNAKES

Using the same game-board, each player now plays his own colour, and may play on any space where no more than two adjacent spaces are occupied by that player's colour. The longest snake of one colour wins. Will you allow a snake to eat its own tail? (Are rings to be allowed?)

Encourage children to explore the topological features of hexagonal tessellations, by inviting them to devise more variations of Hexa.

18

CONTRAST

Here, the children gain experience of a triangular grid, and many simple games can be devised for this board, too.

Cattle Drive, Hexa and Contrast are played on square, hexagonal and triangular tessellations respectively. Can children think of other shapes suitable for making a game board? Can they combine two different shapes in one tessellation?

How many ways are there to produce a game board (tessellation of the plane) containing (1) all identical regular shapes, (2) two kinds of regular shapes (3) repeated shapes of any kind ? The answers to the first two questions will of course be found to depend on the corner angles of regular polygons and whether an exact number of them sum to 360 degrees. The children should soon realise, however, that there are an unlimited number of tilings in the last category.

When children colour the game-boards they have made, how many colours are required for square, hexagonal and triangular grids so that no adjacent spaces are the same? This puzzle offers a simple introduction to the famous map-colouring problem (What is the minimum number of colours needed to colour any map so that no adjacent countries are the same?)

Several Simple Games exploring the Idea of Parity

SQUEEZE

TWINS

HOSTAGE

These games should encourage children to investigate the relationship between alternate moves and the number of spaces available.

19

SQUEEZE (and TWINS)

This is a trivial game, but it enables a child to explore the conditions for winning, to record conclusions and to suggest rule changes.

TWINS

This is a little more complicated, and explores a rather different kind of game. How might the first player move to ensure a win? (Take 2 & 3 or 10 & 11 and whatever the second player does, the first player can then play so that two separate pairs of counters remain for the final moves.)

20

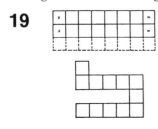

HOSTAGE

This game can be indecisive when two players play cautiously. Some games have an inevitable winning finish (e.g. Minim); some finish, but if played correctly end in a draw (e.g. Noughts & Crosses). Yet others are open-ended unless the rules disallow endless repetition of moves (e.g. Chess).

In Hostage, a diagonal move (effectively two orthogonal steps in one move) can change the advantage of play dramatically – just as a change between even and odd numbers of spaces was

A Further Selection of Short Games

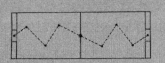

HANDBALL

TWO ACROSS

LAST ACROSS

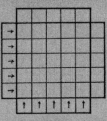

MU TORERE

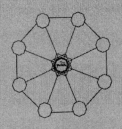

21

HANDBALL

One may save enough points to prevent a score, but this may also prevent one from scoring. In this game, each player should attend to the strategy his opponent is using and make his decisions accordingly. A record should be kept to avoid arguments – and this is useful practice in subtraction.

22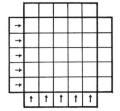

TWOS ACROSS (and NINES)

Played thoughtfully, this little game can be a battle of wits. Does the first player to move have an advantage? Does it pay to move one piece across and off the board quickly? Does it ever pay to move backward?

NINES

A development of Twins, with a second dimension and a good opportunity for children to consider strategy.

23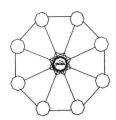

LAST ACROSS

A development of Twos Across.

24

MU TORERE

An intriguing little game from New Zealand. This version (with the two players' counters alternating round the ring at the start) is more satisfactory than the more usual starting layout with all of a player's counters adjacent. In the latter case, an extra rule is needed to prevent an instant win – that a counter may not be moved to the putahi if it has friendly counters adjacent on both sides.

Trapping Games

ARREST

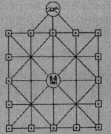

THE REBEL

HASAMI SHOGI

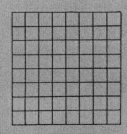

TRAPPER

ARREST

A newly devised game to introduce a series of games in which the trapping tactic occurs (e.g. Hasami Shogi, The Rebel, Trapper).

25

Two black counters pursue one white counter. For how many moves can the white counter remain free? In version 2, each player has two counters, and attempts to arrest first one, then the other opposing counter. In Version 3, orthogonal moves and traps are required, and corner traps

26

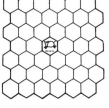

THE REBEL

A more complex traditional game, in which different forces are opposed. As to which player has an advantage. . .? It is much more difficult to be sure in a complicated game like this.

If the Rebel moves wisely, he can reduce the opposing force by four in his first two moves. A time limit can be agreed – The Rebel wins if he is still at liberty when time runs out.

27

28

HASAMI SHOGI

These Japanese games are usually played on the spaces of a portion of a Go board (unlike Go itself, which uses the grid intersections). Our first version involves both short-term objectives (captures) and a long-term aim (a line of five), whilst the second calls for destruction of the opposing force. Some children will discover that counters in blocks of four are safe from capture. With cautious players this can be a long game.

29

TRAPPER

This is a version of the traditional Tibetan game Ming Mang. Trapper permits capture of more than one counter at a time. No jumping moves are allowed.

The most advanced of all the trapping games is Go. For children, a quarter-sized board is appropriate, but slightly simplified rules may also be needed.

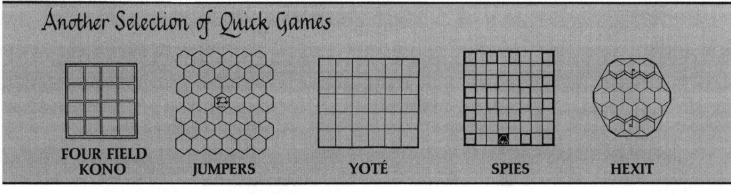

Another Selection of Quick Games

FOUR FIELD KONO   **JUMPERS**   **YOTÉ**   **SPIES**   **HEXIT**

30

FOUR FIELD KONO

Children will enjoy the unusual mode of capture in this little game, and the tactics that this calls for.

31

JUMPERS

One may allow a point to be scored for each counter taken except the last, which scores five. To aid recording of moves and analysis of strategies, the grid may be labelled.

Jumpers may be played as a Solitaire.

32

YOTÉ

A traditional African game, Yoté has a capture rule which makes for rapid wins.

33

SPIES

An entertaining little game based on the idea of n-1; in each round, one spy cannot find anywhere to hide, and is captured.

34

HEXIT
Simplified Draughts on a hexagonal matrix.

More Traditional Games

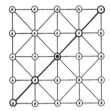

ALQUERQUE   **BULL-DOGS**   **KUNGSER**   **COWS and LEOPARDS**

35

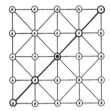

ALQUERQUE
Another game which has been traced back to Ancient Egypt, although this is a Spanish version. Twelve-man Alquerque is a 'jeu forcé', which means that offered captures must be taken, and a missed capture allows the opponent to huff (remove the piece which could have made a conquest).

Peralikatuma (from Sri Lanka) is played with very similar rules on the Cows & Leopards board, with twenty-three men each and three centre points vacant at the start of the game.

36

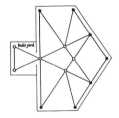

BULL-DOGS
This little game is included as an introduction to tactics used in the more complex traditional games which follow.

Have the dogs a winning advantage? What happens if careless moves allow the bull to dispatch one or more of the dogs? Children may discover that the bull can change the whole pattern of play by one sideways move in his pen. . .

37

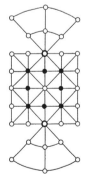

KUNGSER
Cows and Leopards and Kungser are two games with different settings but basically similar rules. Do the children notice this, and the affinity with Fox & Geese?

38

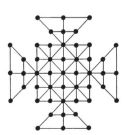

COWS and LEOPARDS
In virtually all board games, there is an advantage (or disadvantage) in playing first. This is true even of Chess; but of course, the more complex a game is, the less influence this factor is likely to have over the result.

Not surprisingly, most board games are played with matched opposing forces. It is difficult to devise a well-balanced game between two opponents whose sets of counters differ markedly in number, power or location. Such games usually reveal a built-in advantage for one of the contenders, as is the case with Fox and Geese. This imbalance may be remedied by alternating roles in successive games, but often it will not become apparent at all until strategies have been well-explored.

A handicapping procedure is traditional for Go players, in order to achieve close-fought contests, and this approach may be appropriate for other games, too.

The Puzzles

Teachers may find the selection of activities which follows useful for individual children and for small groups co-operating in problem-solving.

39

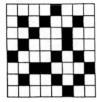

SQUARE IT

The solution is simple, once one has realised the limited numbers of ways in which eight squares can be marked out.

Rotate this matrix until a solution appears.

MR SHAREM-FAIRLEY

40

Children will have difficulty in solving this puzzle by trial and error. What strategy could shorten the search? We are told that the four pieces are identical, yet it is obvious that they cannot be very simple shapes, and reflective symmetry cannot provide the solution.

Square 6,6 has a mill – Let it be in share A. The other corners can be tentatively allotted to B, C and D, working clockwise. It now appears that the mill adjacent at 6,5 belongs to B, and equivalent squares can now be allocated to A, C and D.

The square at 5,6 must be in A... progressively the rotationally symmetrical pattern emerges.

41

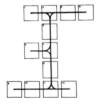

ALL CHANGE

Here is a twelve-move solution: (Can you do better?)

7→8   3→7   6→3   2→6   5→2   6→5   8→6   7→8   6→7   4→6   7→4   8→7.

However, if any colour may be moved, here is a ten-move solution:

6→8   2→6   5→2   2→1   8→5   5→2   3→5   7→3   4→7   1→4.

42

SHUNT

This is much more difficult. Here is a thirty-move solution – Can you do better?

2→6   11→2   12→5   6→12   5→11   2→8   1→6   8→1   11→2   10→5

9→8   12→9   8→10   6→12   5→11   2→8   3→6   4→5   1→4   5→1

8→3   11→2   10→5   6→10   5→11   2→8   1→6   8→1   11→2   6→11

43

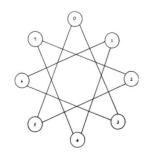

OUTLINE

Only four moves are needed, as shown.

44

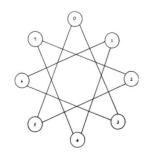

STAR TRACK (and PENTAGRAM)

An example solution is as follows:

6→3   1→6   4→1   7→4   2→7   5→2   0→5, leaving 0 empty.

A practical approach involves first filling the star with seven counters and playing the game in reverse, noting the moves.

Star Track uses an eight-pointed star, with a single track linking all the points. This puzzle offers an introduction to 'clock arithmetic' and finite number systems, and its star track can be described a Modulo 8 with linking operation + 3 (or – 5). There are eight points spaced round a circle, and every third (or fifth) point is joined to form a single continuous track.

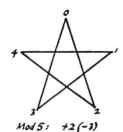

Mod 5: +2 (-3)

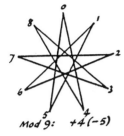

Mod 9: +4 (-5)

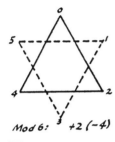

Mod 6: +2 (-4)

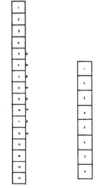

Can the children find any more star patterns with single tracks? Any modulo will produce a single track with the operation + 1 (or − 1), of course, but often the linking operations tried will lead to several interlaced but separate tracks. They may eventually find that Star Track can be played on a number of networks:

Mod 5	+ 2 (− 3)	Mod 9	+ 2 (− 7) or + 4 (− 5)
Mod 7	+ 2 (− 5) or + 3 (− 4)	Mod 10	+ 3 (− 7)
Mod 8	+ 3 (− 5)	Mod 11	+ 2 (− 9) or + 3 (− 8) or + 4 (− 7) or + 5 (− 6)

etc. . .

It may be realised why certain combinations of numbers produce multiple tracks. If the linking operation uses a factor of the modulo, tracks quickly return to their starting points. Modulos with few factors have more distinct 'full tours' – Mod 11 has four such routes, whereas Mod 12 has only one (+ 5 or −7).

Children will enjoy stitching star tracks on card discs. Every time a new track is started from an unused location, a different colour can be used.

PENTAGRAM is a closely related puzzle which apparently orginated in Ancient Egypt; it is still played in Crete and in India. Place a counter on an unoccupied point, move it in a straight line over a second point (which may be occupied) and on to a third (vacant) point, where it remains. Repeat until only one point is vacant. Now try to empty the board by lifting a counter over an intervening piece to a space, removing the piece jumped over. Continue . . . until only one counter is left.

Solutions: Slide the counters successively into the numbered positions. Note even numbers at points, odd numbers on inner pentagon. To remove: 9 jumps over 3, 8/5, 7/1, 6/9, 2/5, 8/1, 10/7, 4/1.

BREAK-AWAY and FOUR-BY-TWO

Quite easy to solve, these problems invite a search for the quickest solutions. Examples are give here – Can you better them?

Break-Away 6, 7→13, 14;   9, 10→6, 7;   13, 14→9, 10;   10, 11→3, 4.
To restore to starting squares: 7, 8→10, 11;   3, 4→7, 8.
Four-By-Two   4→7;   6→2;   8→5;   3→1.

FROGS

As the children investigate this puzzle with increasing numbers of counters, a symmetrical pattern should become apparent:

No. of counters of each colour	Pattern of moves	No. of moves
1	W B W (or B W B etc.)	3
2	W B B W W B B W	8
3	W B B W W W B B B W W W B B W	15
4	W B B W W W B B B B W W W W B B B B W W W B B W	24

If n is the number of counters of one colour, the formula for calculating the number of moves is $(n + 1)^2, - 1$, or $n^2 + 2n$. This pattern could be plotted on a graph. . .

CIRCLES OF HANOI

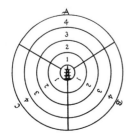

Our version of the well-known Tower of Hanoi puzzle offers opportunities for several mathematical explorations – making a model (experimenting with a simpler form of the problem); making generalisations; exploring symmetries; noting isomorphism (comparable mathematical patterns). . .

Children could tabulate the minimum number of moves and movement patterns for the puzzle, using increasing numbers of counters. This is probably best done in pairs, with one partner recording the moves.

45

46

47

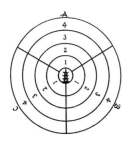

No. of counters	Pattern of moves	No. of moves
1	1	1
2	1 2 1	3
3	1 2 1 3 1 2 1	7
4	1 2 1 3 1 2 1 4 1 2 1 3 1 2 1	15

Now the children are in a position to devise a formula and predict the moves for a five-counter problem ('Double the last number of moves, and add one' – or 'Two, raised to the power of the number of counters, minus one').

The puzzle very rapidly grows more time-consuming – What aspect of the formula causes this to happen?

A similar pattern to this can be observed on an old (Imperial measure) ruler subdivided into halves, quarters, eighths . . . of an inch:

Look also at the binary system:

Decimal No.	Binary No.	Counting from the right, position of final 1 digit in Binary No.
1	1	1
2	10	2
3	11	1
4	100	3
5	101	1
6	110	2
7	111	1
8	1000	4
9	1001	1
10	1010	2 and so on.

Children may plot on a chart the number of counters against minimum number of moves, and discover the exponential curve.

There is a rule of thumb which produces least-moves solutions. Shift the counter in the smallest ring every alternative move, and always in the same direction round the circle. On the other move, make the only move possible.

Children may discover that counters in odd-numbered rings always move in the same direction, and counters in even-numbered rings the opposite way. If one is playing with an odd number of rings, the first move indicates the sector in which all the counters will be assembled, but playing with an even number of rings, the counters will assemble in the sector not chosen for the first move.

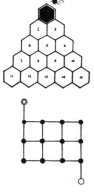

BUZZ OFF
A solution: 4 over 2   11/7   6/3   4/5   13/8   15/14   10/6   12/13   14/9   4/5   6/3.

CAPTURE
Try to minimise the number of steps taken.

DISCO
A perfect solution leaves one counter in the centre, but let children simply try to better their previous attempts. Number spaces to aid recording.

Your comments or suggestions relating to any of these games will be welcomed by the Authors.

TARGET   A game for two or three players
Addition Target : Choose a number between 11 and 20. Each
player places a counter in turn, and the numbers are added
together. The player whose counter exactly hits the target, wins.
Subtraction Target: Subtract each number 'played' from the
starting figure, until exactly zero is reached.

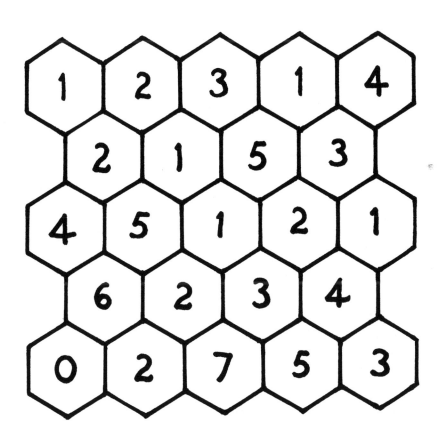

When you are good at this game, play TOTAL or SUMMITS.

TOTAL   First player chooses a number between 15 and 30; this is the target. Players take turns to place a counter, building up a string of connected numerals, and keeping a running total. Player reaching exact target wins; player exceeding target loses. No space may be used twice.

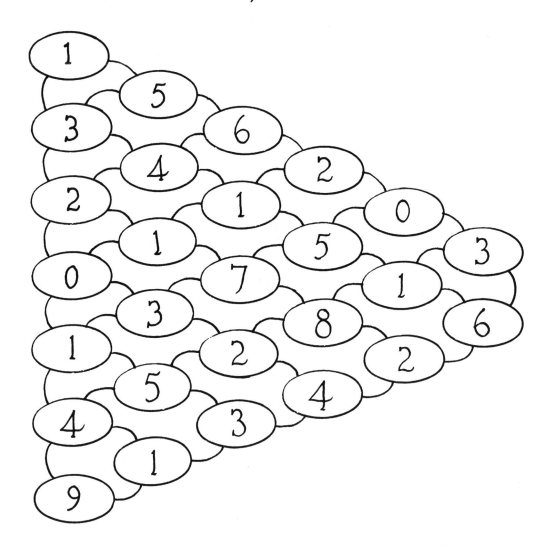

SUMMITS

Players agree on a sum to be obtained; this should be more than 10 and less than 30. First player places a counter on a numeral in the right-hand pattern. Second player uses the lefthand pattern. The sum of the two numbers is noted. Now each player takes turns to move his or her counter one space, and each number is added to the total. Player who manages to reach exactly the agreed sum, wins. Player who cannot help going over this number, loses.

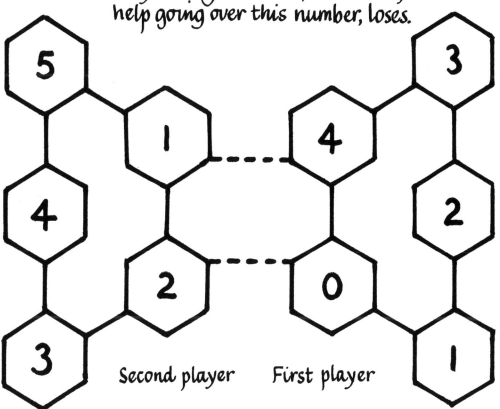

Second player   First player

Version 2   Players may also use the dashed links to cross into the other pattern. In this version, a player may block his opponent's play in one direction, perhaps forcing him to go over the agreed number.

Summits may be played as a Solitaire, recording moves and running totals.

SERPENT   Place counters on the four
black sections. Players take turns to slide
a counter 1, 2 or 3 spaces along the snake's
pattern of dark triangles.

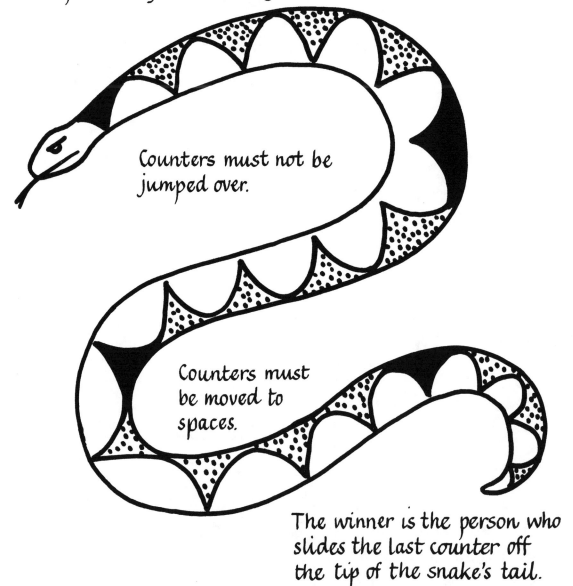

Counters must not be
jumped over.

Counters must
be moved to
spaces.

The winner is the person who
slides the last counter off
the tip of the snake's tail.

MINIM

Twenty-five counters are arranged as shown.
Players take turns to remove one or more counters from any
straight line, provided that there are no empty spaces
between the counters chosen.
The last player to take a counter, loses.

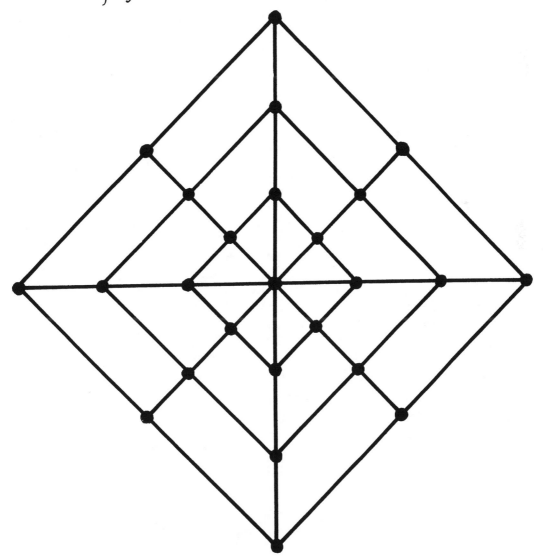

You can easily devise different versions of this game.

WARI

Four beans [counters] are placed in each pit [space]. Players each take six pits on one side. They take turns in sowing the beans from any one of their own pits one by one into the next few spaces clockwise round the board.

If the last bean falls into an opponent's pit and brings the total in it to 2 or 3, those beans are won and are taken off. When there are no beans left on one side, the game ends. The winner is the person who has won more beans.

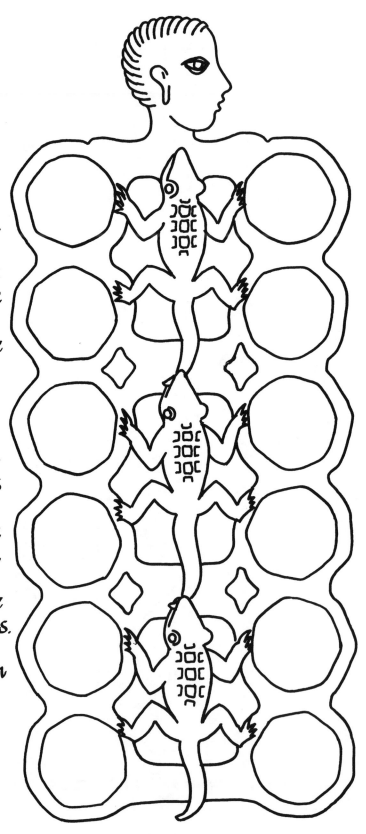

ACHI

The aim is to make a line of three of one's own counters orthogonally [along row or column] or diagonally [from corner to corner]. Each player has four counters, and takes turns in placing a counter on any vacant intersection [a point where lines meet].

If all counters have been placed without a win, each player in turn may slide one of his/her own counters along a line to the vacant point ~ until someone does win. If a player is unable to make a move, he/she must miss that turn.

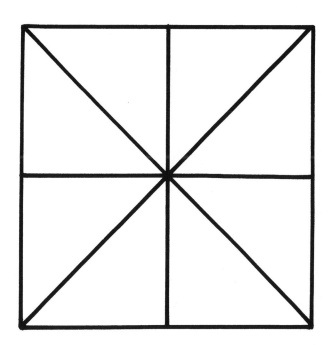

STAR

The aim is to make a straight line of three of one's own counters. Each player has four counters, and takes turns in placing a counter on any vacant black spot.

If all counters have been placed without a win, turns continue, with each player picking up any one of his/her own counters and placing it on the vacant spot.

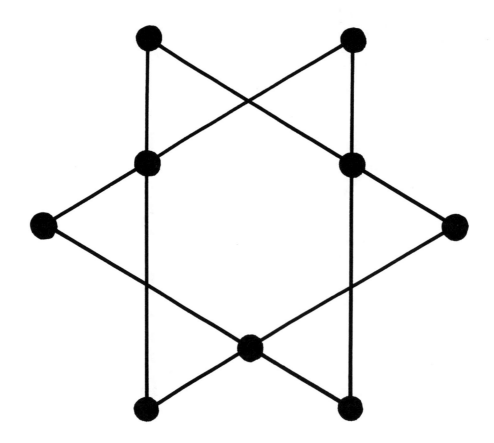

NINE MEN'S MORRIS

Each player has nine counters of his own colour.
Turns are taken to place a counter. When all counters are placed,
a turn consists of moving a counter to an adjacent vacant point,
trying to make a 'mill' [Three counters in a line].
On making a mill, a player removes one of his opponent's counters.
When a player is reduced to two counters, or cannot move, he loses.

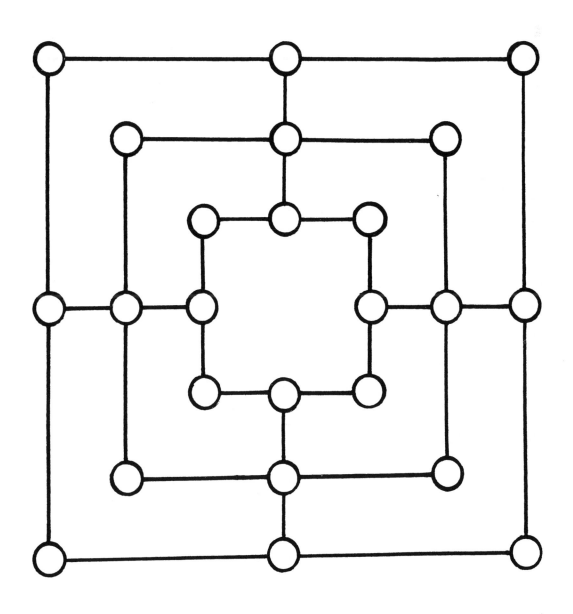

POINT FOUR

Each player should have 25 counters of his or her own colour. Black plays a counter on to a <u>point</u> [intersection], and players take turns until one player completes an uninterrupted line of four of his colour, orthogonally or diagonally.   Version 2   Form a square of four points. In this version the square may be of any size,* or as set.

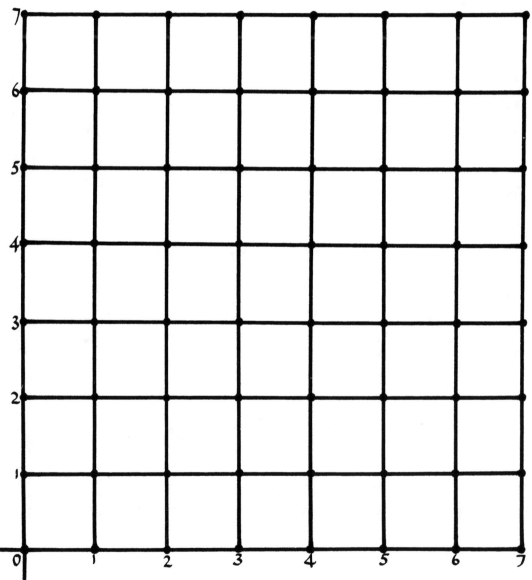

*Other counters may lie within the square formed.

10

BOTTOMS UP!

Each player in turn places a counter of his or her own colour on to the lowest available space in any column. The first player to achieve an unbroken line of four [orthogonally or diagonally], wins. In Version 2 a player may use his move to remove one of his counters from the bottom row, and all the remaining counters in the column concerned move down one place.

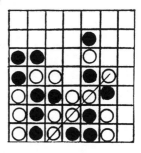

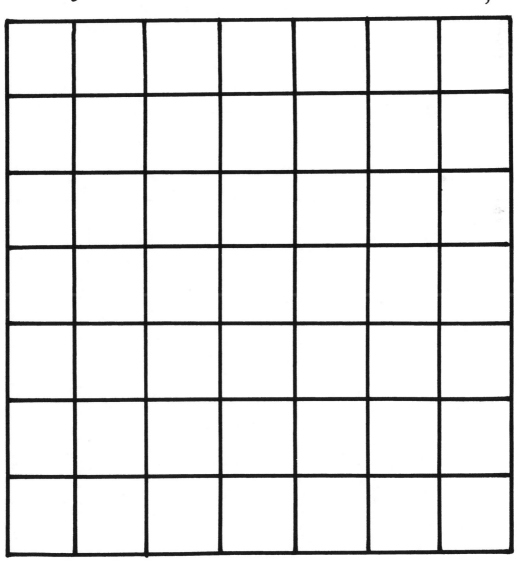

INTERRUPT

Each player has a supply of counters of his or her own
colour. Players take turns to play a counter on to an
intersection [black spot], until one player succeeds in
completing an unbroken line across the board. Only those
links shown on the board may be counted.

Black constructs a line linking top and bottom, whilst
White tries to complete one linking left and right.

Version 2. After playing ten counters, a player moves one
at each turn to an adjacent point.

← White →

← Black →

12

EXCHANGE KONO   A Korean game

Each player's counters are arranged as shown. Players take turns to move a counter one space diagonally on to a black spot, until one player has occupied his opponent's starting positions. There are no jumps or captures.

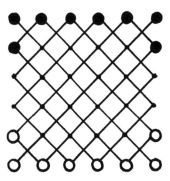

Version 2   A piece may leap diagonally over any other piece to a vacant spot immediately beyond. Chain jumps are also permitted.

A PARLOUR GAME   Spider moves first. Moves are alternate,
one space at a time, stopping at the dots.
Can the insect escape by reaching the window frame before the
spider can catch it?

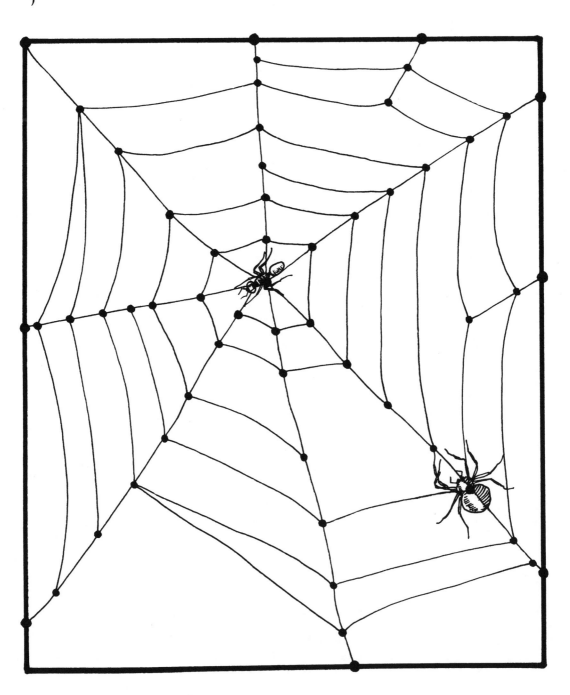

CATTLE DRIVE   A form of 'Fox and Geese'

The three drovers <u>should</u> succeed in catching and trapping the runaway bull... but can they? All moves are diagonal; bull moves first and he may move forward or backward, but drovers must always move forward. If the bull crosses the board, he wins.

FOX and GEESE   A Viking game

In this version from Iceland, there are thirteen geese, placed as shown. The fox is placed on any vacant point. Geese have first move. Moves are then alternate, along a line to an adjacent vacant spot, but the fox may kill a goose by jumping over it to a vacant point. The geese win if they trap the fox, but lose if the fox makes this impossible by killing so many geese. Version 2: This time the geese must not move backward. Fox tries to slip past them to reach the back row.

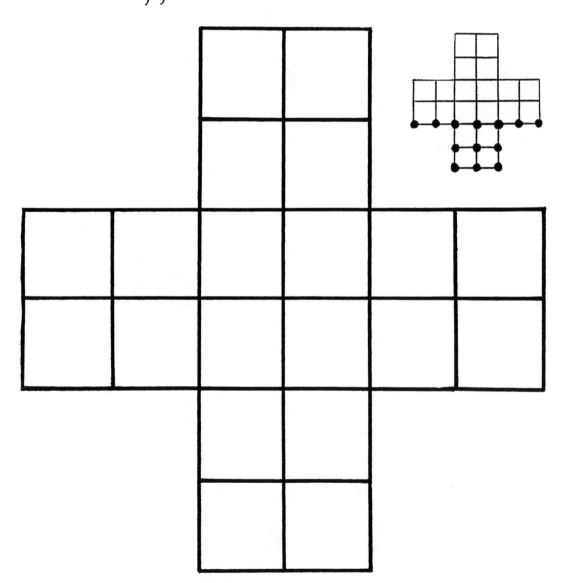

HEXA

Many games can be adapted to play on a hexagonal matrix. Here is a simple introduction: Players take turns to place a counter so that not more than one adjacent hexagon is already occupied. The last person able to play, wins.

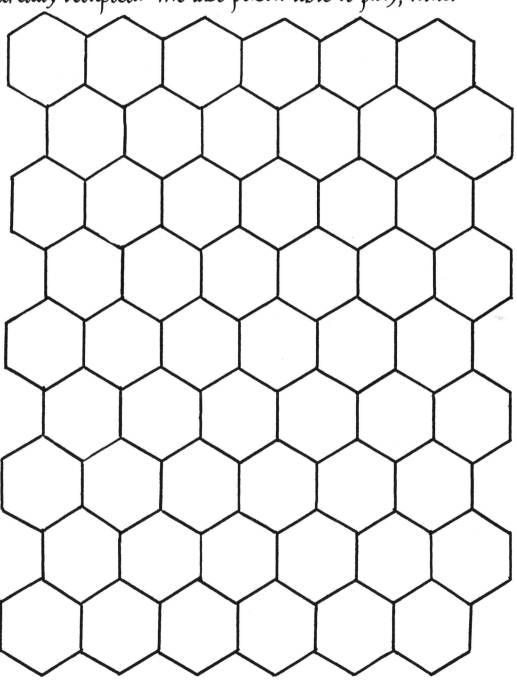

CONTRAST

A game for two or more players, which may be played with either two or three different colours of counter. Players take turns to place a counter of any colour. No counter may be placed in a triangle adjacent to one already occupied by a counter of the same colour. Any player unable to find a move, is out of the game. [Triangles touching only at a point may contain the same colour].

Two simple games

SQUEEZE   Each player has two counters. Black moves first.
Moves are forward or backward only, with no jumping.
Player who cannot move, loses.
Does the first player have an advantage?
Try the game again with <u>three</u> rows of eight cells, three
counters each.   Try the game with rows of <u>seven</u> cells.
*What have you discovered?   Can you invent a rule to improve
the game?*

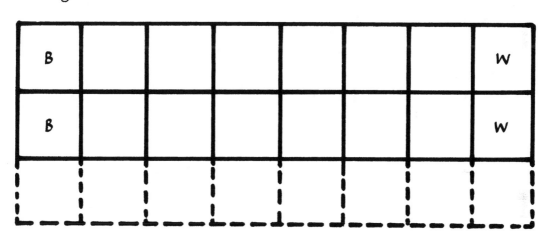

TWINS   Place a counter on each square. Players take
                         turns to remove adjacent pairs of counters.
                         Last to play, wins.

Now play the game in reverse, <u>placing</u> pairs.

HOSTAGE   A chase round a corridor!

Black begins with two men at the squares labelled 1, and White has two men at 2. The winner is the first to trap [and thus capture] one or both of the opposing men.   Each player in turn moves a counter one square forward or backward along the corridor, except that, where indicated, each player is allowed a
diagonal move.

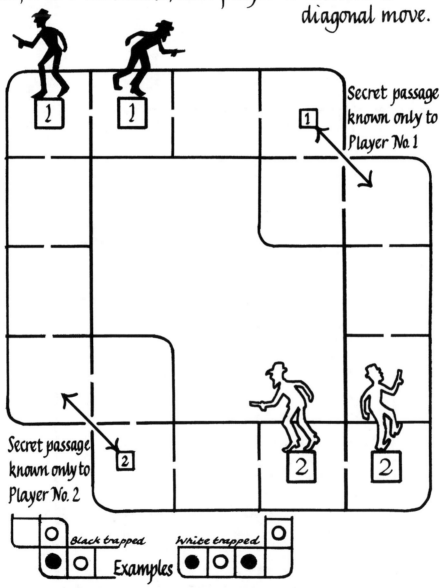

Secret passage known only to Player No.1

Secret passage known only to Player No.2

Black trapped   White trapped   Examples

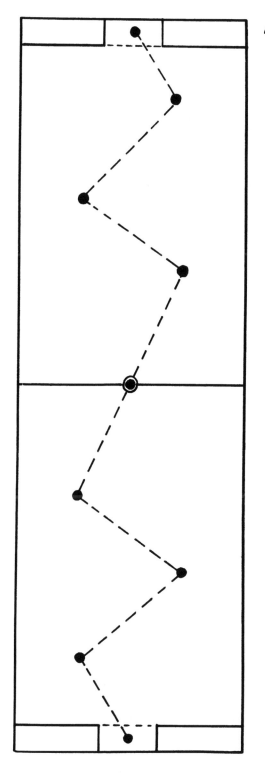

HANDBALL

Place a counter on the centre. spot. Players close fists, and then simultaneously show up to ten fingers. Player showing higher number moves ball one place towards goal.

Players need to be cautious, because each may show a total of only 50 fingers before the next kick-off. If both players show the same number, these are counted in the 50 but the ball is not moved.

TWOS ACROSS

Opposing counters are placed as shown.
Players take turns to move. A counter may
be moved forward, backward or sideways,
but not diagonally.
First player to move both of his counters
across and off the board, wins.

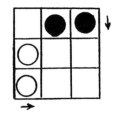

Investigate winning strategies. Investigate the games of
Threes Across [Four Field Kono Board] and Fours Across [Five Field Board]
        4×4 grid   5×5 grid

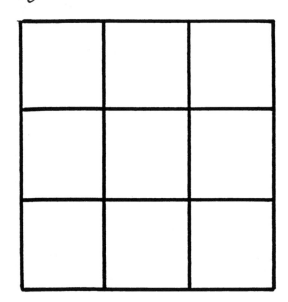

NINES

Players take turns, playing one, two, or three counters
into a row or column on the board [not a diagonal].
The last person able to play, wins.

Investigate a game where only diagonal placings are allowed

Investigate the game of removing counters from a full board.

Investigate the game of SIXTEENS [4×4 board] and
TWENTY-FIVES [5×5 board]

Investigate winning strategies for all of these games.

LAST ACROSS

Each player has five counters of his own colour, placed on the arrows. Moves are alternate, and there are no captures. While one player moves his counters across the board, the other moves his down the board. Last across loses.   Version 1 : Forward moves only.

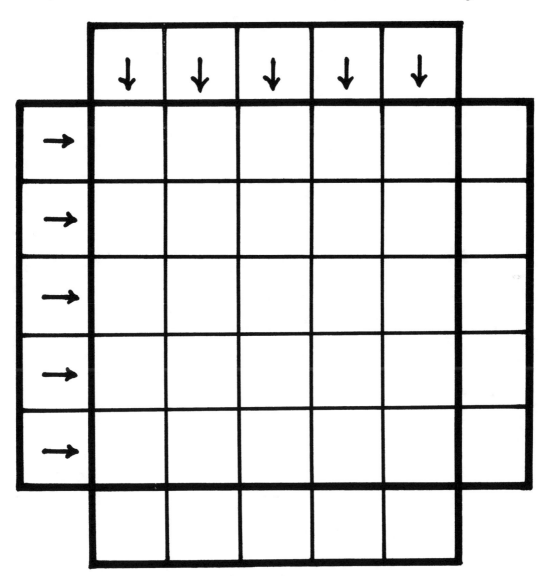

Version 2 : Forward and sideways moves are permitted.
Version 3 : It is also fun to allow jumping over single counters, although no captures are made.

MU TORERE   A Maori game ~ from New Zealand

Each player begins with four counters arranged
alternately in the outer ring. Each player tries
to block the other from moving.
Move: One space round the ring, to the putahi
or from the putahi. There are no captures.

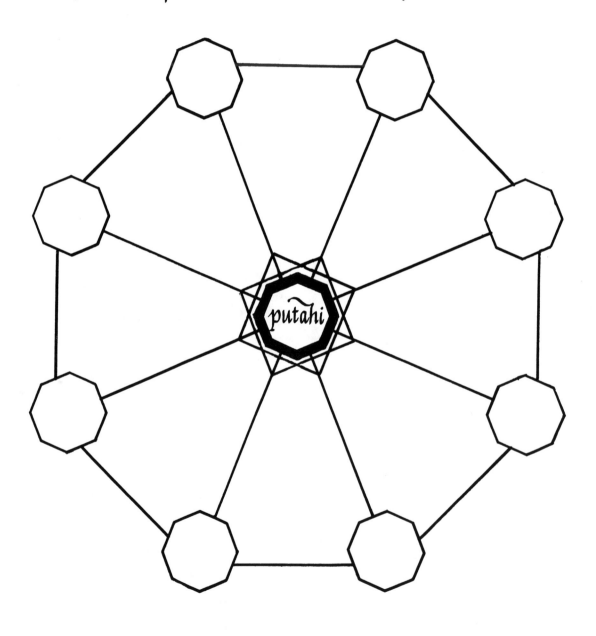

putahi

Arrest!

The player with two black counters tries to trap the white counter.
Moves may be one space in any direction [orthogonal or diagonal].
The white counter is 'arrested' if the black counters are beside
it on opposite sides. White has first move.

Version 2: Each player has two counters, and tries to trap
first one, then the other, opposing counter:

starting position

White trapped

White trapped

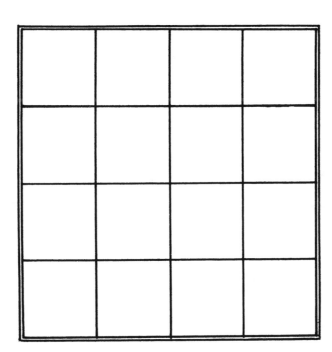

The REBEL — a Chinese game

Sixteen soldiers try to catch the Rebel! Rebel moves first, beginning in his stronghold; soldiers are based in the sixteen outer squares. Soldiers may go anywhere except into the stronghold or the mountains — where only the Rebel can go. Players take turns to move one space in any direction along a link. Rebel can kill two soldiers by moving into a space between them. Soldier tries to make a move which leaves Rebel between two soldiers, or blocks the Rebel from moving.

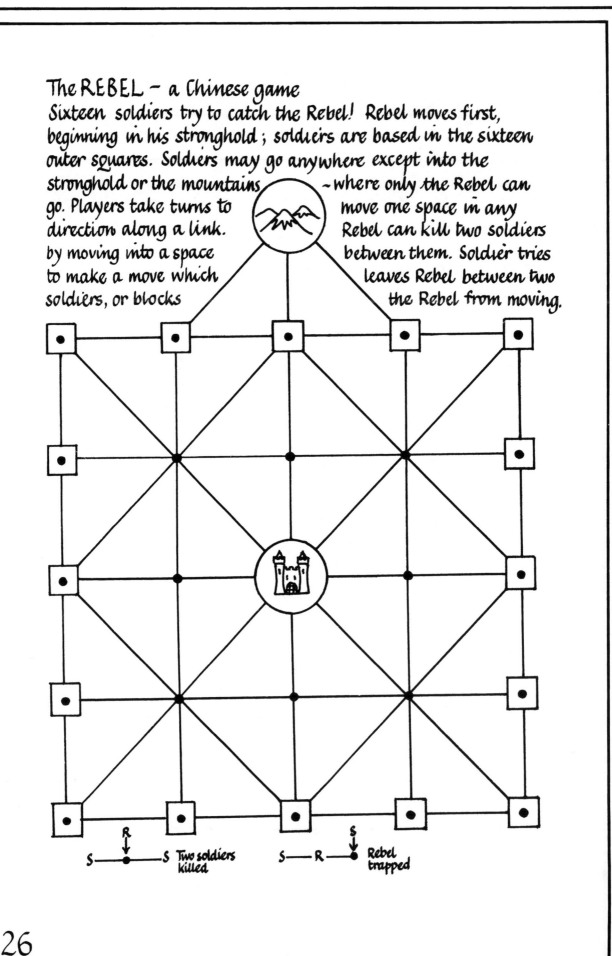

S ——— R ——— S Two soldiers killed

S — R — S Rebel trapped

HASAMI SHOGI

Version 1   Each player begins with 18 counters of his or her own colour filling the back two rows on one side of the board. The aim is to complete a straight line of five counters of own colour [in row, column or diagonal] outside the two 'home' rows. Moves are like those of a Castle in Chess ~ any number of spaces along row or column ~ but a counter may instead jump over an adjacent counter to the next space. No diagonal moves are allowed. Captures are made by trapping an enemy counter between two home counters in row or column, but a piece may safely be moved into a gap between enemy counters.

Black   White

HASAMI SHOGI

Version 2 Each player begins with nine counters on the back row of his side of the board. The aim is to capture all of the opposing counters. Moves are like those of a Castle in Chess ~ any number of spaces along row or column~ but a counter may instead jump over an adjacent counter to a space immediately beyond. No diagonal moves are allowed. Captures are made by trapping:

but this is a safe move:

TRAPPER

Opposing counters are arranged as shown. Enemy counters [one or more in a continous line] are to be trapped between two home counters. Those 'squeezed' are replaced by home counters. A counter may safely be moved into a gap already existing - trapping __must__ involve the placing of an attacking piece. Moves are orthogonal [rows/columns] any number of spaces - like a castle in chess.

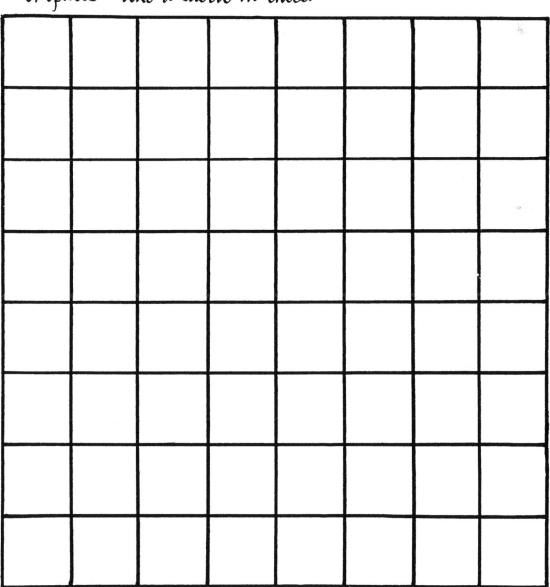

FOUR FIELD KONO

A Korean game. Each player starts with eight counters, as shown below. The capture rule is unusual: Jump over one of your own counters to land directly on an enemy piece, which is taken. The player whose pieces are all lost or trapped, loses the game. Every move is *orthogonal [not diagonal], and <u>one</u> space unless capturing.

* along row or column

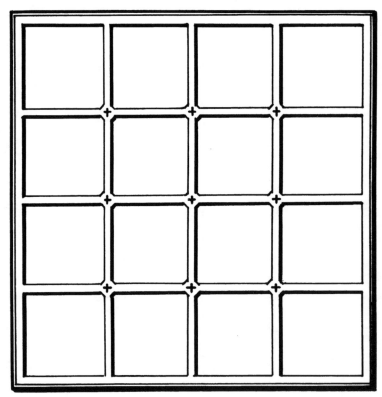

Jumpers

Fill every hexagon with counters, except the centre. Players take turns to 'jump' over a counter into a space immediately beyond. The last player able to play, wins. Of course, each counter jumped over is removed. Chain jumps are allowed if there is a space between each 'victim'.

Solo Jumpers   A Solitaire game ~ for one person

Play the game by yourself.

Try to have only one counter left!

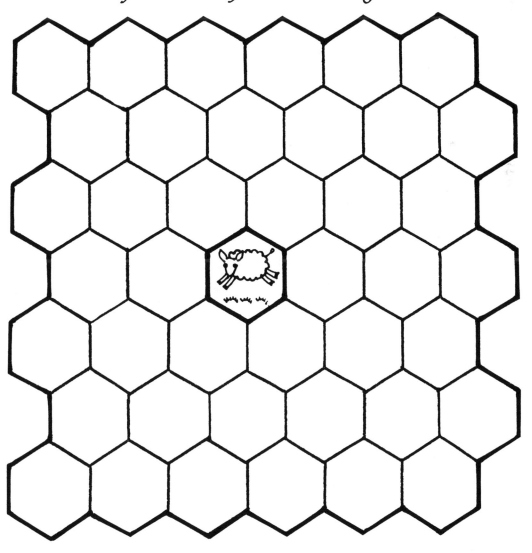

YOTÉ   A West African game

Players take turns to place twelve counters of their own colour, or to move a counter already placed. Moves and captures are orthogonal; a move is one space, and a capture is made by jumping over an enemy piece to a space immediately beyond. A player who makes a capture may remove an extra counter. Chain jumps are not allowed.

[Orthogonal means along a row or column, but not diagonally]

SPIES

Two players with six counters of their own colours [or three players with four counters, or four players with three each] take turns to place a spy [counter] in the central meeting room. A trap has been set, and as soon as all have arrived the alarm sounds! The spies rush to hide in the twelve secret hiding places, but one place is already occupied.
The player whose spy is caught out in the open, loses.
Move: One space in any direction, or jump over any other spy to a space just beyond. Chains of jumps are allowed.

This game can be repeated ~ with one less spy and one less hiding place, until only one player has any spies left.

HEXIT

Each player has seven counters in the back rows of the board, leaving a central row of five spaces. The aim is to occupy the city of the opposing force [by moving three 'home' counters into the opposite back row]. Black moves first. A move is one space forward into an adjacent hexagon. A capture may be made by jumping forward or sideways over an enemy piece to a space just beyond. Chains of jumps are allowed. Offered captures must be taken (jeu forcé) If a player is left with only two counters, the game is lost.

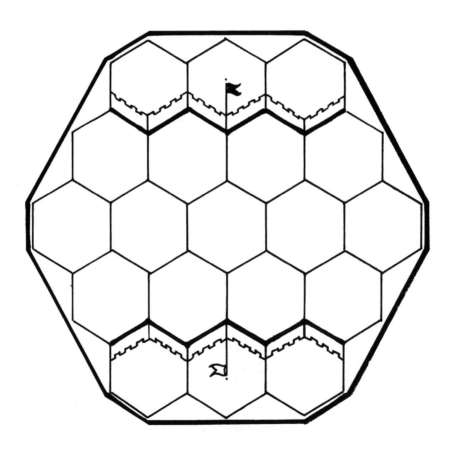

ALQUERQUE

A Spanish game, brought from Africa by the Moors as 'El-quirkat'

Player A and Player B place their twelve counters each, leaving the centre space empty. The aim is to capture the opposing pieces by jumping over, as in Draughts. Chain jumps are allowed, and offered captures must be taken. The normal move is along one link to a space. A player loses if he has no counters or if all moves are blocked.   Version 2: No 'backward' moves.

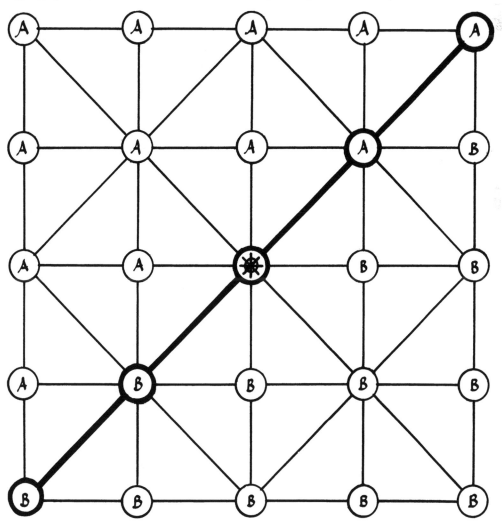

BULL ~ DOGS

The gate is open, and the bull escapes into the field. How can the farmer's seven dogs drive it back to its yard? The bull makes the first move from his yard, and the dogs start from the black spots. The bull may move along a line to the next space, or toss a dog off the field by leaping over it to a space directly beyond. In his move, the farmer may move any one dog one space along a line.

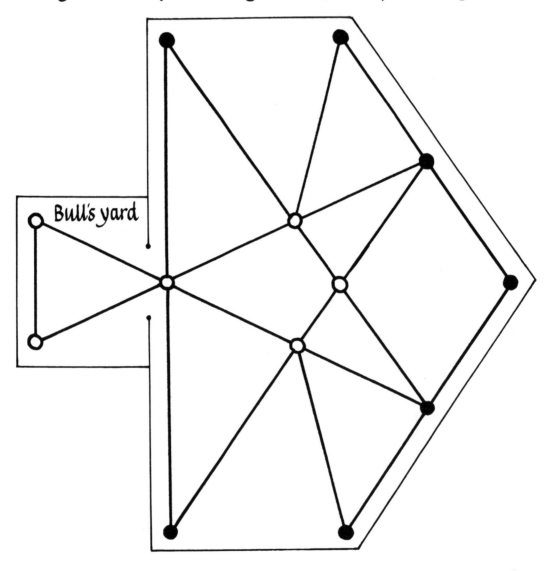

Bull's yard

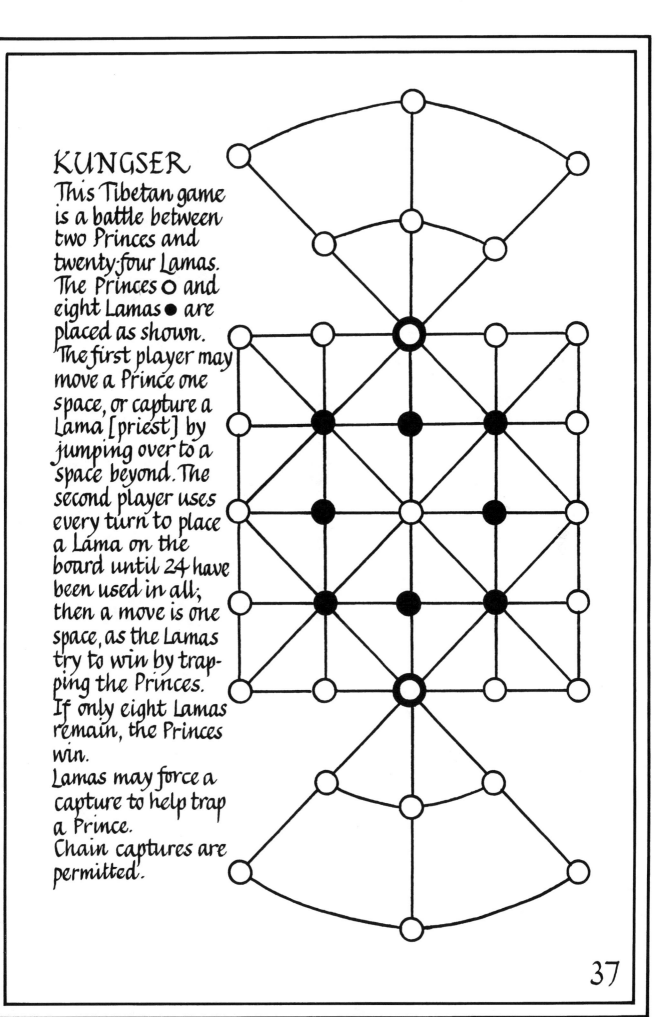

KUNGSER

This Tibetan game is a battle between two Princes and twenty-four Lamas. The Princes O and eight Lamas ● are placed as shown. The first player may move a Prince one space, or capture a Lama [priest] by jumping over to a space beyond. The second player uses every turn to place a Lama on the board until 24 have been used in all; then a move is one space, as the Lamas try to win by trapping the Princes.

If only eight Lamas remain, the Princes win.

Lamas may force a capture to help trap a Prince.

Chain captures are permitted.

From Ceylon comes the game of COWS and LEOPARDS.
Leopards kill cow by jumping over it to a space just beyond ...
Cows trap leopard by blocking all moves. Cows win if they
can trap both leopards...   First player places a leopard, second
player a cow; second leopard is placed, and second cow. The
leopards now attack, but second player uses 24 turns placing
cows ~ only then can cows be moved. Normal move for cow or
leopard is from one spot to an adjacent vacant spot, along a line.

Two leopards
versus
twenty-four cows...

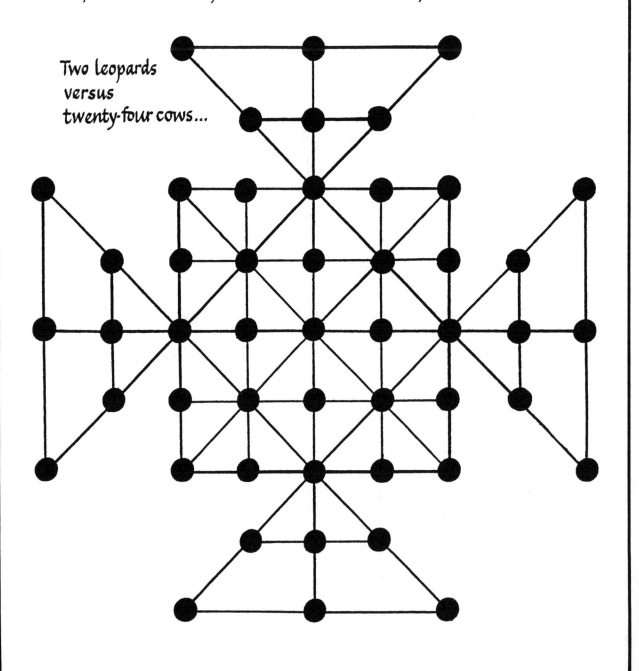

SQUARE IT   A puzzle for one.

Divide this square into eight smaller squares so that each one contains at least one of the small black squares.

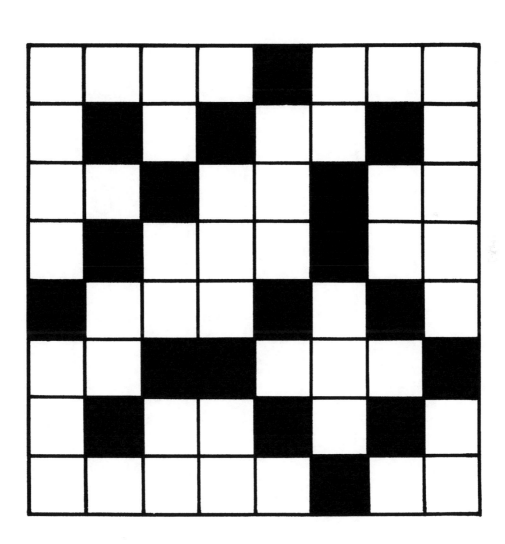

MR. SHAREM-FAIRLEY   A tricky puzzle for one.

Mr Sharem-Fairley is retiring, and he has decided to share his land and property equally between his four children. Can you divide the large square area into four parts identical in size and shape, so that each part includes one house, one well, and one windmill?

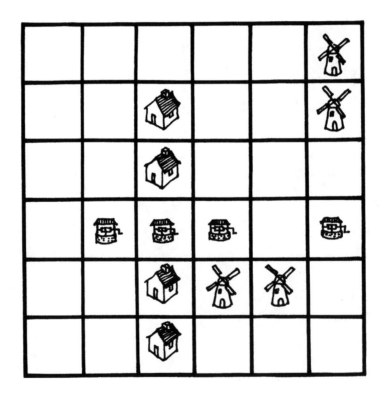

ALL CHANGE   A puzzle for one

Exchange the positions of the black and white counters in as few moves as possible.

Moves are one square in any direction [including diagonally] to a vacant square, but black and white must be moved alternately.

Record your moves.

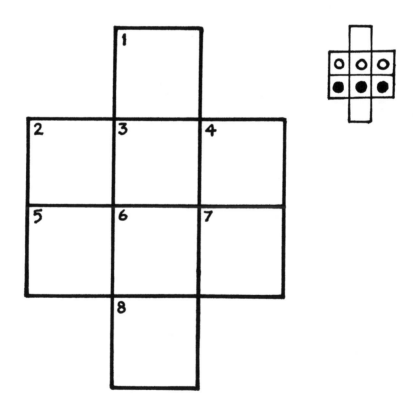

SHUNT   A puzzle for one

Arrange counters as shown.
Change over the black and white
counters by moving them along
the track and by using the
siding.   Record your moves, and
try to take as few as possible.
Only one counter may occupy each
square.

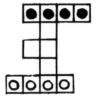

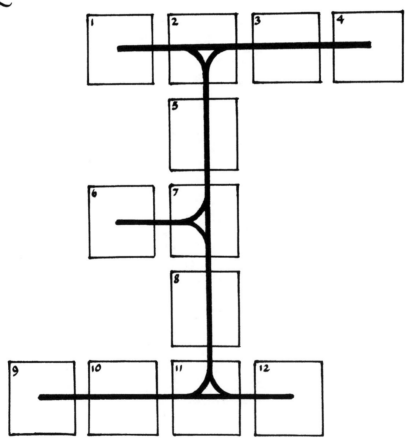

OUTLINE   A puzzle for one.

Begin with five counters placed as shown.
Slide counters along diagonals until no two
counters are in line diagonally, vertically,
or horizontally.
Try to reduce the number of moves. The distance
from one cross·over point to the next counts
as one move.

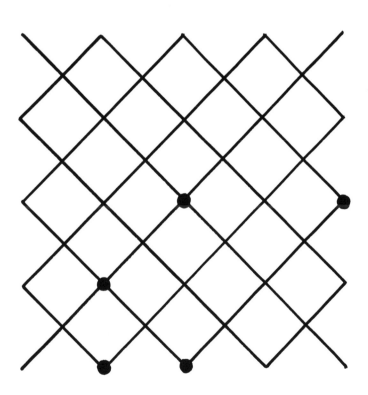

STAR TRACK   A puzzle for one.
Place counters on seven of the eight points, by following
this rule: A counter must not be placed on a vacant point
directly, but must first be put on another unoccupied but
connected point and moved along the 'star track' joining
the points. Thus, to cover point 1, one must start from 4 or 6.
Record your moves.
Find a way to leave point 0 vacant.

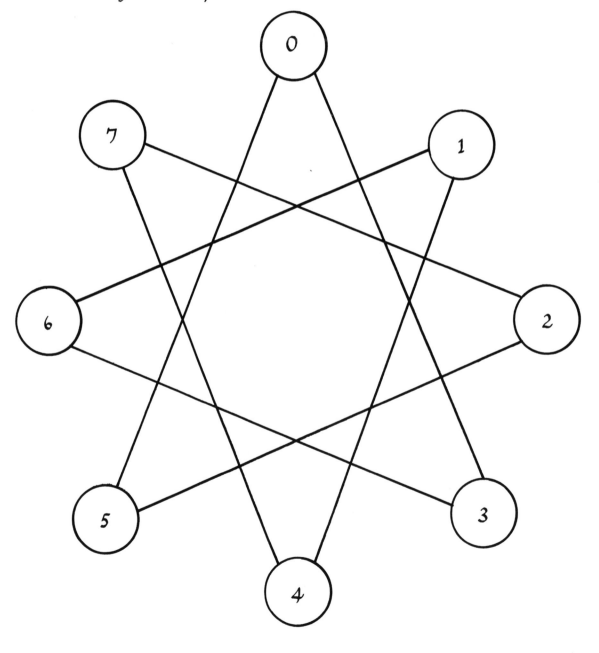

44

Two twinning puzzles...

BREAK-AWAY

Black and white counters are arranged as indicated.
Moving an adjacent <u>pair</u> of counters at a time to
a <u>pair</u> of spaces, sort out the colours to leave four
black on one side and four white on the other.

What is the least number of moves needed?
Record your moves using the numerals on the squares.

You could try this puzzle with extra counters.

1	
2	
3	
4	
5	B
6	W
7	B
8	W
9	B
10	W
11	B
12	W
13	
14	
15	
16	

FOURBYTWO

Place a counter in each
cell. Make four pairs
of two counters.
A counter must jump
over two counters to
land on a single one,
when a move is made.

Record your moves like
this: 2 → 5 .....

1
2
3
4
5
6
7
8

45

FROGS

Four counters (black) are placed in the four lefthand squares; four more (white) are put in the righthand squares. The squares remaining are left empty. The aim is to change the counters over.

Moves: Slide one square to a space OR jump over one counter to a space.

If you can solve the puzzle, note down the colour of each counter you move - B or W.   Is there a pattern? What is the least number of moves needed?

If you can't solve it very easily, try the puzzle with just one counter on each side, in the squares marked: 5 and 7. Record the moves.   How many?

1 Empty

2

3

4

5

6 Empty

7

8

9

10

11 Empty

Then try with 2 counters each side, 3 counters each side, and 4 each side..... Can you do it now? If you can, guess how many moves are needed for 8 counters each side. Make a playing board to test your theory.

What kind of pattern have you noticed?

CIRCLES of HANOI   A puzzle for one

Place a counter on each of the numbers 1 to 4 in
Sector A. Move the counters in the fewest possible
moves so that they all finish in Sector B.
Rules : Counters are moved one at a time, each round
its own ring to either of the other sectors. No counter
may be moved <u>from</u> a sector or <u>to</u> another sector in
which there is a counter nearer to the centre.
Record your moves.

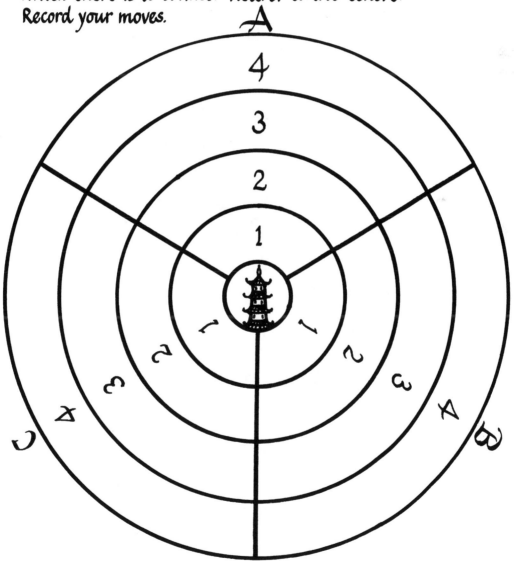

BUZZ OFF   A Solitaire

Place a counter on each space except the top one.
A bee [counter] jumped over escapes from the hive.
A bee reaching the top hexagon also escapes.
Can you leave the hive empty?

Example 'jump' – shaded counter is removed.

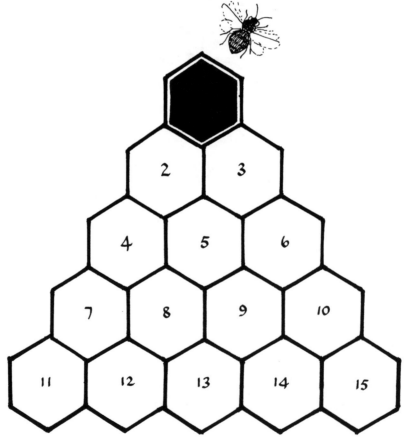

CAPTURE A puzzle for one

Many puzzles can be devised for this board, on which twelve black counters and one white one are placed. The aim is to have only the white counter left, and to take as few moves as possible.

Version 1 Any counter may be moved to a vacant space 'next door' or it may jump over a counter to reach a space. The counter jumped over is removed.

Version 2 A chain of jumps made by one counter is allowed as one move.

Version 3 Jumps round corners are also allowed.

Version 4 Black counters may be moved, but only the white counter may jump over [and capture].

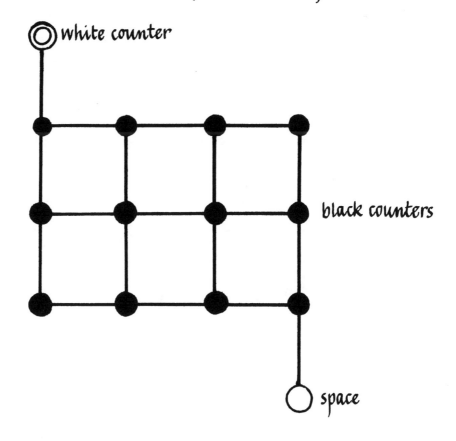

white counter

black counters

space

DISCO   A Solitaire

Place a counter on each space except the central one.
A counter is removed when it has been jumped over.
Try to leave as few counters as possible.

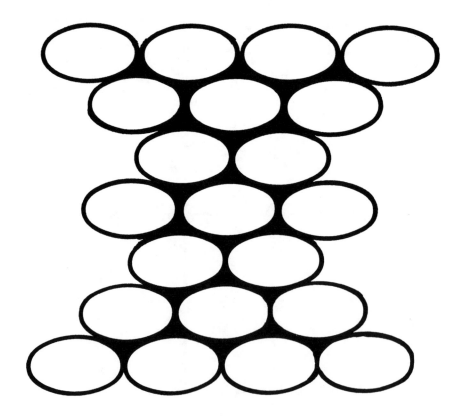